KU-220-284

BMA

FAMILY DOCTOR GUIDES

Depression

Dr Greg Wilkinson

Series editor: Dr Tony Smith

Dr Wilkinson is senior lecturer in the General Practice Research Unit, Institute of Psychiatry, London, and honorary consultant psychiatrist at the Bethlem Royal and Maudsley Hospitals.

EQUATION

Published by Equation in association with the British Medical Association

First published 1989

© British Medical Association 1989

British Library Cataloguing in Publication Data

Wilkinson, Greg, *1951-*
  Depression
  1. Man. Depression
  I. Title II. Series
  616.85'27

  ISBN 1-85336-110-0

Picture acknowledgements

Photographs by John Rae; Cartoons by Raymond Fishwick. Diagram by David Woodroffe.

Equation, Wellingborough, Northamptonshire NN8 2RQ, England

Typeset by Columns of Reading
Printed and bound in Great Britain by
The Bath Press, Avon

10 9 8 7 6 5 4 3 2 1

Contents

1 Introduction

Depression is a word with many shades of meaning. Most of us feel sad or miserable sometimes; life is full of problems, disappointments, losses and frustrations that can only too easily cause unhappiness and despondency. Generally, however, our low moods are normal, healthy reactions that are short lived and fairly easily shaken off. In fact, if we look hard enough we can always find something in our life to blame for the way we feel—our job, children, finances, relationships—and nowadays there seems to be a tendency to call all unpleasant emotions 'depression'. But if we were to examine our feelings more closely we would probably find they could be described more accurately as anger, frustration, jealousy or fear! Sometimes, however, we feel low or despairing for no apparent reason or our mood is depressed out of proportion to the circumstances, and no matter what we do we can't seem to shake it off. Depression of this kind is an illness that needs medical help.

Learning to cope

This book is all about depression. It discusses the symptoms and the different types of depressive illness, the possible causes and the treatments available. Don't expect to find too many clear and final answers, however, as doctors don't know everything about people and their emotions—even when they are well. Nevertheless, we have tried to give useful information, advice and practical help. And remember that although our knowledge may be incomplete, there are many successful treatments available.

2 Recognising depressive illness

Most low moods are temporary and understandable. Depression becomes a problem when there is no apparent reason for it or when it persists long after the stress that caused it has disappeared or been resolved. Depressive illness is a persistent exaggeration of the everyday feelings that accompany sadness. It is a disturbance of mood that varies in how severely it affects different people and in how long it lasts, that often recurs and is associated with a wide number of different mental and physical symptoms.

How do you know if you need help?

Depressive illness can creep up on you but you or your close family or friends will usually recognise that you need help when the symptoms become too severe or last too long. Sam, Rosie, and Mr Flynn showed symptoms of depressive illness when they visited their doctors.

Sam

Sam found that he began to feel isolated and lonely, even with friends and family around. He could no longer feel any affection for his family and began to reject their attempts to comfort him. Increasingly he found it difficult to cry and, in any case, tears no longer brought relief.

Gradually his energy waned and he lost interest in things: talking and even concentration became an effort. He found himself thinking a great deal about the past, and unpleasant memories returned to upset him. He started to feel restless, agitated and irritable and sometimes became very anxious.

Sam was persistently gloomy: pessimism and hopelessness were ever present.

Rosie

Rosie was miserable, particularly in the mornings. Her sleep pattern had changed, she was finding it difficult to get off to sleep in the evening and she was waking up in the early hours, unable to get back to sleep. She worried increasingly about her health. Rosie's mother had died of breast cancer and she began to think that she would die for the same reason. She was off her food and had lost almost half a stone in weight in the past month. She had taken time off work because she was unable to cope and she began thinking that she was worthless. She kept on feeling guilty at the trouble she caused other people and the 'awful' things she had done. She could no longer bear her husband to touch her.

Rosie criticised her performance as a wife and mother and blamed herself for bringing shame upon her family. Life no longer seemed worth living.

Mr Flynn

Mr Flynn is 60, he has not attended the doctor for over a year. He looks sad and dejected.

Mr Flynn has always been in good health but recently he noticed that his clothes had become loose and was worried to find that he had lost a stone in weight over the past three months. His appetite has gone and he has begun to be constipated for the first time in his life. He now wakes early from an unrefreshing sleep.

He admits to feeling miserable and unwell. Most of the time he lacks energy and concentration, and he is no longer even interested in the television. All this has been developing gradually over the past six months.

As it turns out, Mr Flynn has lived alone since the death of his wife two years ago. They had no children. Mr Flynn's main interest in life had been his work as an engineer in a local components factory. A year ago he was made redundant and has been unable to find work. He feels bitter, humiliated, and useless.

In discussion it comes out that Mr Flynn has been neglecting himself. His personal hygiene is poor and his breath smells of alcohol. He admits that he has begun to drink more heavily—half a bottle of whisky a day—and is living on takeaways.

When asked if he sometimes thinks that it would be nice to go to sleep and not wake up again, he turns away and begins to cry.

Symptoms of depression

The Table overleaf lists the possible symptoms of depression. It is a fairly daunting list, but fortunately most people do not suffer from the more severe forms of the illness that include hallucinations and delusions as symptoms. Typically, the symptoms are misery and unhappiness but with little reason to account for feeling so low spirited. Sleep is disturbed and you may find that you wake early in the morning and are unable to get back to sleep. Your appetite may be poor, with the result that you lose weight. You may, however, eat more and gain

Possible symptoms of depression

Mood
Sadness
Misery
Gloom
Despondency
Anxiety and tension
Lack of enjoyment
Lack of satisfaction
Loss of affection
Weeping
Mood swings
Temper
Irritability

Thinking
Loss of interest
Lack of pride in oneself
Sensitivity
Feelings of uselessness
Feelings of apathy
Feelings of nothing mattering
Inability to cope
Difficulty making decisions
Shame
Hopelessness
Self-blame
Worthlessness
Forgetfulness and inability to concentrate

Drive
Wish to escape
Withdrawal
Feeling of being in a rut
Activities seem dull or meaningless
Desire to seek refuge

Physical
Feeling run-down
Tired
Aches
Pains
Loss of appetite
Loss of weight
Sleep disturbance
Loss of sexual appetite
Fatigue
Inability to relax
Palpitations and sweating
Agitation
Physical slowing
Constipation

Judgement
Delusions: typically of guilt, worthlessness, & bodily illnesses
Hallucinations: often of voices saying negative things, eg 'You are dying of cancer, AIDS' etc.

weight but this is less usual. Some people suffer from constipation and there is often a sense of being unwell. You may feel you can't cope with everyday life—everything is an effort and you get tired very quickly. Nothing gives you pleasure any more—you lose interest in work, hobbies, sex, and in your personal appearance.

Symptoms may be misinterpreted

The tiredness and other physical symptoms may make you think that you have some physical disease and even your doctor may search for some physical cause for the way you are feeling.

Restlessness and agitation

You may feel that life has battered you into defeat. Tears may flow or there may be dry eyed suffering. Tension and anxiety may enter the picture making you worried or touchy, and the slowness or apathy may, at times, be replaced by outbursts of anger or bad temper. Sometimes depression makes people restless, unable to keep still or settle to anything.

False friends

Some depressed people turn to alcohol, cigarettes or non-prescription drugs in the belief that these may help them to cope with or deaden the pain. Unfortunately this is not the case and these substances only make things worse. Alcohol not only causes social, family and emotional damage but is also a cerebral depressant drug that provokes or prolongs depression.

Effect on family and friends

Family and friends may be very worried and frustrated because nothing they do or say seems to help. This frustration may mean that they lose sympathy, they want to tell you to pull yourself together, they become impatient...and they feel guilty about their own emotions.

Severe illness

Up to this point the experience and behaviour of someone with a depressive illness is comprehensible to the average person, even though the mood is much lower than seems to make sense. If the illness is of a more severe type, however, it can be more difficult for others to understand. Self criticism and feelings of worthlessness may become an overwhelming guilt. Small lapses in the past may be exaggerated into mortal sins, into crimes that have led to shame, disaster and even death. Convinced of their 'badness', sufferers may hear voices telling them that they deserve to die or that they have some terrible disease.

Suicide

It is difficult for someone who is not severely depressed to understand the distress, despair and the sense of guilt and impending doom suffered. But even when depression is not this intense, suicide is still a risk. We will look at suicide more closely in Chapter 5.

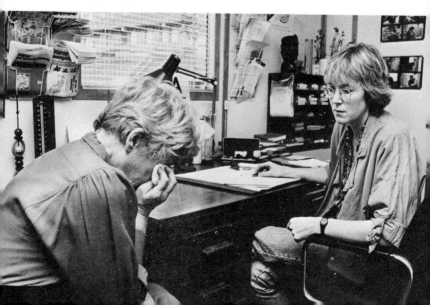

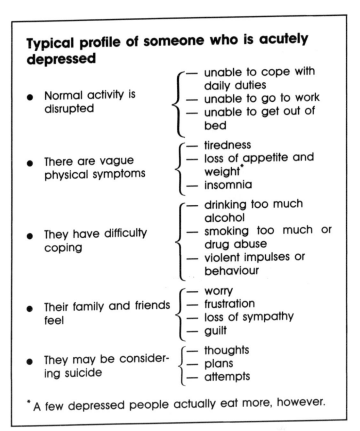

Typical profile of someone who is acutely depressed

- Normal activity is disrupted
  - unable to cope with daily duties
  - unable to go to work
  - unable to get out of bed

- There are vague physical symptoms
  - tiredness
  - loss of appetite and weight*
  - insomnia

- They have difficulty coping
  - drinking too much alcohol
  - smoking too much or drug abuse
  - violent impulses or behaviour

- Their family and friends feel
  - worry
  - frustration
  - loss of sympathy
  - guilt

- They may be considering suicide
  - thoughts
  - plans
  - attempts

* A few depressed people actually eat more, however.

Four conversations

Judith
'I don't know, I just seem to feel generally depressed and I don't feel as if anything around me is real, everything looks artificial. I'm physically fine. It's just that I just want something to help stop this feeling I have of just wanting to cry all the time.'

Archie
'I am feeling a bit run down, I keep feeling tired. I am sleeping well, but I feel tired all the time and a bit depressed. I got up this morning and I just couldn't face going to work.'

Elaine

'Well I just wanted to sit around, and I just seemed to be crying for no reason. I think I was feeling guilty about Michael. When I talk about him I fill up. I think such a lot of him. To think that he's sort of handicapped in this way and children are so cruel. And he feels so bitter about himself, you see. I don't know how to explain it, having so many children and everything all right and then he turns out like this, I felt as if I was being paid back for deserting my first family.'

David

'A fortnight ago I started having migraine again after a couple of years of not having it. And I started to get sort of palpitations and pins and needles, and a sort of funny feeling in my stomach and travelling up to my throat. I tried to eat something but I couldn't, I didn't feel like eating, I didn't want to eat. In fact I couldn't be bothered with doing anything.'

Why do symptoms of depression begin?

There may be several factors to consider in depression and we will look at these more closely in Chapter 4. Symptoms usually begin, however, in response to:

- The amount of stress you are under—and remember that several minor problems may be as important as one major problem;
- The kind of person you are—your personality make-up, constitution, and hereditary factors are important.

Mrs Bradshaw

Mrs Bradshaw is 27, married with three children aged 4 and 2 years and 6 months, and has recently moved from Newcastle, where she has lived all her life, to a council estate in London. She makes an urgent appointment with her new doctor. When she arrives at the surgery she is carrying her youngest child followed by the other two. She is tense and weepy.

She tells the doctor that she has not felt well since arriving in London. She feels drained, moody and irritable, is sleeping poorly and has frequent headaches. She feels unable to take any more.

It emerges that her husband is not supportive and spends most evenings in the pub. He is unemployed and they moved to London to seek employment. She feels resentful of her husband's lack of help. He in turn criticises her for her loss of interest in sex—which she puts down to exhaustion.

Mrs Bradshaw has few acquaintances and no friends in the area—she wishes she were back home beside her family, but there seems no prospect of this.

How long does depression last?

Without treatment, depression that is well established tends to last for a period of months, occasionally perhaps even years. Remission nearly always occurs, however, particularly in younger people. About a third of sufferers have only one attack in their lives but in the rest depression returns, with a second episode occurring two to five years after the first. In older people, the episodes tend to become more frequent and to last longer. If depression is severe, relapse is likely in about three quarters of people affected, and about a third will have long-standing, persistent or fluctuating symptoms and some social difficulties. It is a very sad fact that about 15% of severely depressed people eventually commit suicide.

How common is depressive illness?

Depressive illness is very common but its extent varies in different places and in different groups. Surveys show that 20% to 30% of the population may suffer symptoms of depression in the course of one year. Fortunately, most people have mild depression but about one person in 20 will have a moderate or severe episode.

As a rough guide, severe depression affects 3% to 4% of us, but only 20% of those affected see their doctor, of whom only 50% are treated by a psychiatrist. Only one person in 50 with a depressive illness needs hospital treatment.

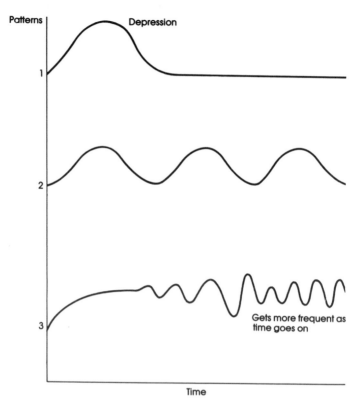

Patterns of depression

So who gets depression?

- Women are about twice as likely as men to suffer from depression, but the proportions are about equal for severe or recurrent depression;
- Among women the incidence and prevalence varies with age, the highest rate being in the 35 to 45 years age group;
- The rate of depression increases with age in men;
- Depression is most common in the highest and lowest social classes;
- Married people have lower rates than single people, except perhaps for teenagers;
- A small group of people suffer from 'seasonal affective disorder' and have recurrent episodes of depression in the winter months. An even smaller group suffers recurrent summer depressions.

3 Types of depression

Depressive illnesses range from mild to moderate to severe. Milder forms are often called 'neurotic' or 'reactive' depression by doctors, while the more severe types of the illness may be referred to as 'psychotic' or 'endogenous' depression. Fortunately milder illnesses are far more common. In addition to these names, doctors use a variety of confusing terms to classify different types of depression, but none is entirely satisfactory.

In this chapter we will look at the various classifications of depression and at particular events such as bereavement and childbirth that are closely linked with depressive illness. If you find the section on classifying depression a little heavy going, don't worry, you can skip on to the second part of this chapter.

Depression classified according to cause

Depression may be classified as 'reactive' or 'endogenous'.

Reactive depression

In reactive depression, the symptoms are thought to be caused by an external stress such as bereavement or unemployment, whereas in endogenous depression, symptoms seem to occur independently of such outside factors. With many depressed people, however, this distinction does not seem to be clear cut. Stressful life events can often be shown to precede both types of depression and there are not two distinct groups of symptoms.

Endogenous depression

Psychiatrists decide a patient has endogenous depression if they show signs of sadness, social withdrawal and have many of the following symptoms:
- Loss of sex drive;
- Anorexia or weight loss;
- Physical and mental slowness or restlessness and agitation;

- Early morning wakening;
- Feelings of guilt;
- Lack of pleasure in anything;
- Feeling lowest in the morning with mood improving as the day goes on;
- Persistent low mood that does not change even when something pleasant happens;
- Low mood that is different in quality from normal sadness.

Primary and secondary depressions

The aim of this classification is to separate depression caused by some other physical or psychiatric illness or drug or alcohol abuse ('secondary' depression) from depression that does not have these causes ('primary' depression). This classification is used for research rather than treatment purposes.

Depression classified according to symptoms

Depression may be classified as 'neurotic' or 'psychotic' depending on the symptoms. But again the distinction between these is less obvious than doctors would wish, as many people have symptoms of both types of illness and some types of depression (notably endogenous) are neither neurotic nor necessarily psychotic.

Neurotic depression

Neurotic depression usually follows a distressing experience but is more severe than the experience merits. Sufferers are often preoccupied with the emotional trauma that preceded the illness—for example the loss of a loved one, a job, a treasured possession, or an ideal. People suffering from neurotic depression may be agitated and anxious as well as depressed. They may suffer from hypochondria or abnormal fears such as agrophobia but they do not suffer from delusions or hallucinations.

Psychotic depression

Strictly speaking the term 'psychotic' should be reserved for depressive illness associated with delusions and hallucinations, or both.

Manic depressive psychosis

Manic depression is usually a recurrent illness in which there is a severe disturbance of mood. People with this disorder may show a mixture of depression and anxiety but sometimes this may be replaced by elation, excitement and overactivity—the picture termed 'mania'. The mood disturbance may be accompanied by one or more of the following features:

- Disturbed attitude to self;
- Inability to understand what is going on;
- False beliefs;
- Behaviour that is out of character and socially unacceptable;
- Disorders of perception, occasionally including hallucinations.

When these symptoms are present, they are in keeping with the person's mood. Someone who is manic depressive will, for example, believe that they can conquer the world when they are elated but feel like a useless, worthless worm when low and depressed. People who are manic depressive may also have a strong (often unexpressed) tendency to commit suicide.

Distinguishing between the two

Doctors make the distinction between neurotic and psychotic depression not only on the basis of the severity of the depression but also on the other symptoms present and on how disturbed the person's behaviour is. Thus someone with a mild mood disorder may be deemed manic depressive (psychotic depression) if their symptoms match closely the descriptions given above.

Depression classified by the course of the illness

Depression that occurs alone and is not associated with manic illness (the opposite of depression, in which the person is very elated) is known as 'unipolar' depression. In 'bipolar' depression episodes of depression and mania occur alternately or together. There is some overlap between these groups since unipolar depression may include some people who will go on to suffer an episode of mania.

Masked depression

Although depressed mood is a prominent feature in most people with a depressive illness, some may show little evidence of low mood or other symptoms. A diagnosis of masked (or atypical) depression is occasionally made when depression is thought to underlie unexplained physical and mental disorders, such as long standing pain with no apparent cause or hypochondria, or otherwise inexplicable behaviour such as shoplifting in middle-aged women.

Bereavement

The process of grief is a natural and necessary response to an important loss and involves the bereaved person in a gradual acceptance of the reality of the loss, experiencing the pain of grief, severing the ties with the lost person and readjustment.

Phases of grief

There are several phases of grief after loss:

- A period of shock, numbness or disbelief lasting from a few hours to a few weeks;
- Mourning with intense yearning and distress. The bereaved person is likely to show many of the features of depression at this stage, which usually reaches a peak at two weeks but may last for some months. There is a sense of futility, loss of appetite, restlessness or irritability, preoccupation with the deceased (including short-lived hallucinations), guilt and even denial of the fact of death;
- Acceptance and adjustment begin to take place several weeks after mourning has begun and the bereaved person gradually takes a renewed interest in the outside world;
- Resolution of grief is usually seen within the first 12 months but it may take longer than this.

Abnormal grief

Most bereaved people manage to adjust to their loss despite the pain of grief. Sometimes, however, long-standing grief may lead into a depressive illness, but it is often difficult to decide when a normal grief reaction needs medical treatment. Some of us find grieving too painful to bear, in which case few of the typical features of grief will be evident. This is known as 'delayed grief'. Or we may devote all our time and energy to some activity (which often has some connection with the person who has died) to avoid dealing with our grief. This reaction is called 'displaced grief'. Neither of these reactions is abnormal—they are present in some degree in most people—but when they are excessive, they delay the normal process of grieving and can be harmful.

Postnatal depression

Most women experience a period of emotional disturbance sometime within the first 10 days after having a baby, when their emotions feel unstable and they are low and weepy. It often lasts for one or two days and then passes. This is 'baby blues' and not the first sign of postnatal depression.

About two in every thousand childbirths are complicated by the development of a mental illness, however, and three

quarters of these are postnatal depressive illnesses. Postnatal depression may take up to three months or more to develop and can be mild or severe like other depressive illnesses. The symptoms are identical but, in addition, the mother may be over concerned with the health of her baby and her adequacy as a mother. Unfortunately, because of these feelings of inadequacy, mothers may feel guilty about seeking help.

Good prognosis

Postnatal depression is generally relatively short lived and the results of treatment are usually good, but the risk of recurrence after the next pregnancy is about one in seven.

Depression and the elderly

Old age is a time of increasing vulnerability to depression. Sometimes, however, depression in the elderly is masked by physical illness and handicaps such as deteriorating eyesight or hearing, so it is especially important to be aware of the possibility of a depressive illness in an old person.

4 Causes of depression

As in many other illnesses, the exact cause of depression is not known but a number of different factors have been identified that may contribute. There is probably an important genetic element that makes some of us more prone to depression, and unpleasant life events and some physical illnesses help to cause depression because of their psychological and bio-chemical effects.

Genetic factors

While our genetic make-up plays a large part in manic depressive illness, there is no evidence that this contributes to reactive depression, where family environment is the main influence.

First degree relatives (children, brothers and sisters and parents) of people with severe depressive illness have a greater risk (10% to 15%) of suffering from depressive illness than the general population (1% to 2%). The theories about the reasons for this genetic inheritance are conflicting, and the search for 'genetic markers' that indicate a tendency to depression remains unsuccessful.

It is probable that inheritance makes some of us more prone to depression but this has not yet been proved.

Brain and body chemistry

Some chemicals in the brain and body seem to play a large part in controlling our emotions and changes in the amounts of these are found in people with depression. The hormone noradrenaline, that plays a major role in controlling brain and body activity seems to be reduced in those who are depressed. In women, the hormone changes associated with childbirth and the menopause may also increase the risk of depression.

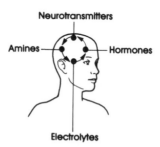

Some chemicals seem to play a part in controlling our emotions.

Body type

Contrary to traditional belief, people who have a rounded and thick-set body type are no more prone to depression than others.

Mood swings and depressive personality

Although at times we all experience fluctuations of mood for no obvious reason, and though some people seem to have more exaggerated 'highs' and 'lows', those with this type of personality are no longer thought to be more prone to depression. Some people have a depressive personality which means that they are persistently gloomy and despondent. This means that they may become socially isolated, reinforcing depression.

Stress

Death of a loved one, loss of a job, moving house, or other major stresses have been implicated in causing depression. Reaction to the stress is often delayed, however, and the depression may come on some months after the event has occurred.

Life events and stress*

Events	Stress rating
Death of spouse Divorce Marital separation Jail term Death of close family member Personal injury or illness Marriage Loss of job	**Highest**
Marital reconciliation Retirement Change in health of family member Pregnancy Sex difficulties Gain of new family member Business readjustment Change of financial state Death of close friend	**High**
Change in number of arguments with spouse Mortgage of over £20 000 Foreclosure of mortgage or loan Change in responsibilities at work Son or daughter leaving home Trouble with in-laws Outstanding personal achievement Wife begins or stops work Begin or end of school Change in living conditions Revision of personal habits Trouble with boss	**Moderate**
Change in work hours or conditions Change of residence Change in schools Change in recreation Change in church activities Change in social activities Mortgage or loan less than £20 000 Change in sleeping habits Change in number of family gatherings Change in eating habits Vacation Christmas	**Low**
Minor violations of the law	**Lowest**

*Holmes and Rahe

Life events

Research has shown that adverse life events tend to cluster in the six to 12 months before the onset of depression. There seems to be an increase in the occurrence of depression after the most stressful types of life events. Threatening types of events bring forward the onset of depression. This research can be criticised, however, for a number of reasons. People with depression, for example, may be feeling very negative and may tend to remember and report more negative events. It is also true that the impact of an event upon a particular person is difficult to predict—some people cope with stress better than others and what stresses one person may not trouble another.

Vulnerability factors in depression

In a study of young, working class women in inner London, the following factors were found to increase the frequency of depression in women who also had experienced a threatening life event or major difficulties:
- Loss of mother before age of 11 years;
- Three or more children under 14 years at home;
- Lack of an intimate confiding relationship;
- Unemployment;
- Other long-standing difficulties.

Not the whole picture

The results of this study have not been fully accepted, however. Vulnerability factors are thought to *increase* the likelihood of depression in the face of adverse life events but they do not *cause* depression by themselves. For example the fact that mild depressive illness is more common in young women in Inner London if they are 'working class' is best explained by being working class increasing the likelihood of their becoming depressed when things go wrong. Perhaps they are less likely to be given the support they need by their families. It is also true that women are more likely to suffer from mild and severe depression than men. We are not sure why this is but it has been suggested that hormonal changes (postnatal mental illness, premenstrual syndrome, the menopause), exposure to more long-standing stress factors and different ways of coping with stress may explain some of this difference.

Some physical causes of depression

- **Neurological diseases**
  - Parkinson's disease
  - Multiple sclerosis
  - Strokes
  - Epilepsy
  - Dementia

- **Malignant diseases**
  - Lung cancer
  - Brain tumours
  - Cancer of the pancreas

- **Endocrine diseases**
  - Hypothyroidism
  - Cushing's syndrome
  - Addison's disease

- **Kidney disease**
  - Kidney failure
  - Kidney dialysis

- **Anaemia**
  - Iron deficiency
  - Folate deficiency
  - B_{12} deficiency

- **Infections**
  - Influenza and post-influenza
  - Hepatitis
  - Glandular fever
  - Brucellosis

- **Side effect of drug treatment**
  - Methyl-dopa
  - Corticosteroids
  - L-dopa
  - Diuretics (water tablets)
  - Barbiturates
  - Reserpine

- **Drug withdrawal**
  - Benzodiazepine tranquillisers
  - Amphetamines
  - Alcohol

The role of physical illness

People with severe physical illnesses or longstanding disabling conditions such as rheumatoid arthritis may well suffer depression as a result. Some conditions, however, also act as specific causes of depression.

Childbirth—not an illness . . . but

The period immediately after childbirth is also strongly associated with the occurrence of symptoms of depression as well as the risk of depressive illness. In most cases this is due to the psychological adjustments necessary after childbirth as well as the loss of sleep and hard work of caring for baby.

Psychological mechanisms

The early psychoanalysts suggest that because depressive illness resembles mourning their causes may be similar. They believed that depression could be caused by loss of a loved one, a treasured object or pet, or of a deeply felt ideal.

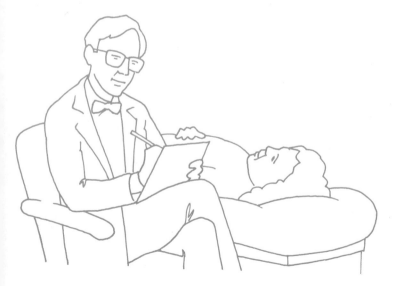

Cognitive theory of depression

Most people would regard gloomy thoughts as a result rather than a cause of depression. Recently, however, it has been suggested that it is the ideas themselves ('depressive cognitions') that are the major cause of depression, or aggravate and perpetuate the condition. Thus someone who has a negative view of him or herself, the world, and the future is more likely to suffer a depressive illness than someone with a more positive outlook. Depressive cognitions can be divided into three types:

- **Thoughts**   eg, 'I'm a failure as a parent.'
- **Expectations** eg, 'I cannot be happy unless everyone likes me.'
- **Distortions**   eg, Drawing conclusions without any evidence for them. 'People don't talk to me because I'm boring.'
  Concentrating on details and missing the important aspects of a situation.
  Drawing a general conclusion on the basis of one incident. 'My work is useless because my boss complained once.'
  Relating bad events to yourself when this is unjustified.

This way of looking at depression is known as the cognitive theory of depression.

5 Suicide and attempted suicide

Most of us have wished we were dead at some time or other—often for no other reason than wanting to make someone else sorry for something they have done to us. But people suffering from depression may feel so low that they seriously consider killing themselves. Suicide and attempted suicide (also known as parasuicide) are overlapping behaviours but as the Table shows, there are some differences— apart from the obvious one.

Features of suicide and parasuicide

Suicide	Parasuicide
Fatal	Non-fatal
Premeditated	Impulsive
Rates falling in recent years	Rates increasing in recent years
Rates increase with age	Rates decrease with age
Commoner in older men	Commoner in young women
Drugs and violence are common methods	Preponderance of drug overdose
Lower and upper social classes	Lower social class
Loss of parent by death in childhood	Broken home in childhood
Poor physical health	Good physical health
Normal personality	Abrupt mood swings or antisocial personality
70% have depression	10% have depression
Social isolation	Social disorganisation

Suicide

Suicide is an intentional act of self destruction by someone who knows what he or she is doing, and the probable consequences. In law, there is no presumption of suicide unless there is *evidence* that the victim intended to kill him or herself (eg a suicide note). The person must also have been mentally capable of forming an intent to kill themselves.

Can you put the idea of suicide in someone's head?

Some people worry that by mentioning the word 'suicide' to a depressed person they may put the idea into their head, thereby increasing the likelihood of such an act. This is simply not true.

How does someone get to this point?

Suicide is usually a feature of severe depressive illness but occasionally even mildly depressed patients succeed in killing themselves. Suicidal thoughts start gradually. At first there may be the feeling that life is not worth living, then later the thought that it would be a relief to go to sleep and never wake up again, or to die, or be killed suddenly. Preoccupation with death increases and becomes persistent and vague thoughts about suicide turn into planning possible methods, culminating in a suicide attempt or suicide.

Important factors

Other factors are also important: suicide is commoner in the elderly, the physically ill, and in those who abuse alcohol, as well as in those who have made previous attempts. In the end, about 15% of people with a depressive illness commit suicide.

How common is suicide?

Although official figures underestimate the number of suicides, the suicide rates in Britain are among the lowest in the world.
- Suicide is the sixth most frequent cause of death after heart disease, cancer, respiratory disease, stroke, and accidents;
- Suicide is the third most common cause of death in the 15 to 44 age group;

- Suicide accounts for about one death every three to four years in a population of 2500.

Causes of suicide

Misfortune, mental illness, and isolation from other people are the main causes of suicide. Well planned social and medical services are the best way of recognising people at special risk and helping them before it is too late. It is known that:
- Virtually all suicides (95%) are mentally ill before death;
- Some 85% suffer from depression (70%) or alcoholism (15%) beforehand.

Medical contacts

Most people who commit suicide have recently seen a doctor for treatment.
- About 80% have seen their GP (three quarters in the month before suicide and half in the week before death);
- Some 25% have seen a psychiatrist (half in the week before death);
- Around 80% have been prescribed psychotropic (mood altering) drugs by a doctor.

Risk factors for suicide

The early detection of risk factors and warning symptoms is vital if we are to reduce the number of people who commit suicide. In particular, there is a strong relationship between suicide and depressive illness.

Attempted suicide

Attempted suicide is a non-fatal act, most commonly involving an overdose of drugs (particularly mood changing drugs) but also including other types of self-injury. Only about 10% of people who attempt suicide seriously intended to kill themselves.

How common is attempted suicide?

- Over 100 000 people attempt to commit suicide in England and Wales each year.
- Three or four people on the average family doctor's patient list attempt to commit suicide each year.

Factors in suicide

Social factors	Illness	Warning symptoms
Male sex	Depressive illnesses	Suicidal thoughts
Age more than 45 years	Alcoholism and drug addiction	Severe depressed mood
High and low social class	Schizophrenia	Persistent insomnia
Separated, divorced, or widowed	Serious physical or chronic incapacitating illness	Noticeable loss of interest
Immigrant	Recent para-suicide (particularly using violent means)	Hopelessness
Social isolation	Personality disorder (moody anti-social)	Worthlessness and inadequacy
Unemployment and redundancy	Organic brain disease (early dementia, epilepsy) head injury	Guilt
Retirement	Family history of alcoholism	Agitation or lethargy
Living in a socially disorganised area such as an inner city		Social withdrawal
Recent bereavement		Anger and resentment
Spring months		Unresolved or deteriorating health or social difficulties
		Self neglect
		Memory impairment

Causes

Most people who attempt suicide are not mentally ill.
Attempted suicide is usually an impulsive response to a social
crisis in someone whose vulnerability has been increased by
alcohol. The main purpose is probably to communicate
distress. People who have attempted suicide have often had a
recent increase in adverse life events, most usually in the
preceding week. These include:

- Quarrels and arguments with spouse, family, or friends;
- Personal physical illness;
- Examinations;
- Court appearance;
- Difficulties with children, finances, work, health, and alcohol;
- A new person at home;
- Family illness.

Medical contacts

Most people who attempt suicide seek medical help beforehand:

- 65% have seen their GP in the month beforehand;
- 35% have seen their GP in the week beforehand;
- 20% have seen psychiatrists in the same intervals;
- 25% have seen a social worker, clergyman or voluntary
  agency in the month beforehand.

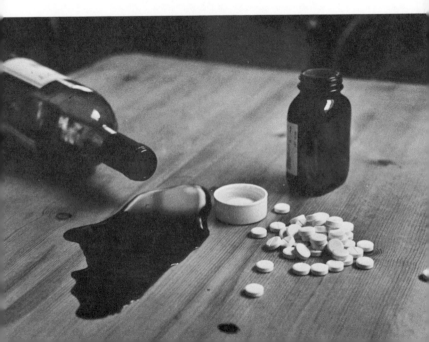

Suicidal intent

About 1% of those who attempt suicide commit suicide within a year of attempted suicide, and 10% commit suicide in the long term. The degree or nature of the drug overdose or injury at the time of the attempt does not help in predicting the eventual outcome, and promises that future suicidal impulses will not be acted upon are unreliable. In determining how serious the attempt was, significance is attached to:

- Risk factors for that person;
- Mental illness (especially depressive illness);
- The recent attempted suicide (especially an extensive wound or a jump from a height);
- Whether precautions to prevent discovery were made;
- Whether the attempt was premeditated or impulsive;
- Absence of precipitating factors.

Risk of repetition

About 15% of those who attempt suicide try to kill themselves again within a year. The risk of a further attempt is strongly associated with:

- Previous episode of attempted suicide;
- History of psychiatric treatment;
- Criminal record;
- Low social class;
- Separation from spouse or partner;
- Previous episode not precipitated by social crisis, drug dependence, or alcoholism;
- Separation from mother at an early age.

Treatment of people who attempt suicide

Most people manage to sort out the family or personal problems that drove them to despair and doctors (with nurses and social workers) can help to resolve the problems by counselling all those involved.

- Virtually all those who attempt suicide are admitted to a medical or attempted suicide unit for appropriate medical treatment;
- Hospital admission is normally overnight, or for 24 to 48 hours.
- Most people who attempt suicide should be assessed by a psychiatrist after they have recovered but before going home, though local policies vary;
- Depending on their physical recovery, someone who has attempted suicide and is mentally ill should be referred for

treatment, either to a psychiatric outpatient clinic or to their GP, preferably within a week of the attempt;

- Some 20% of those who attempt suicide need to be transferred to an inpatient psychiatric unit for detailed assessment and treatment;
- Very occasionally, compulsory admission to a psychiatric hospital under Section 2 of the *Mental Health Act* is necessary, and this will usually be arranged by a psychiatrist;
- Voluntary and social services agencies may be approached to provide support to socially disadvantaged people who have attempted suicide;
- Despite all efforts, a large proportion of people who have attempted suicide will fail to continue with whatever treatment is offered—this is usually because the stress that caused the crisis has been relieved.

Prevention of suicide and attempted suicide

Suicide is a major preventable cause of death, and attempted suicide is one of the most easily identified risk factors for future suicide. Half of those who commit or attempt to commit suicide give some clue of their intention. Other factors that could help reduce the rates are:

- Reduction in toxicity of drugs and poisons;
- Improved medical treatment of those who attempt suicide;
- Improved medical *and* personal recognition and treatment of mental illness;

- Increased access to medical and social services;
- Regular follow up and social support for those at risk;
- Care in prescribing mood changing and other drugs to those at risk, and their close family;
- Provision of more information and advice to those at risk and their family and friends, for example on the use of medical, social and voluntary services, vulnerability following drinking alcohol, and The Samaritans telephone counselling service;

Open 24 hours a day.

The Samaritans

- Improvement of the social and material circumstances of those at risk;
- The impact of risk factors should be reduced;
- Self help groups.

6 Tackling depression

Many people discover their own ways of controlling the symptoms of depression, without the help of doctors or other health professionals. The main questions to ask yourself are:

- Is there anything I can do when I feel depressed that makes me feel better? In general, keep doing it (alcohol and 'false friends' excepted);
- Do any of the things that I do make me feel worse? In general, avoid doing them (if you can);
- Is there anything that I think might help if only I could do it? Try it out, if at all possible.

What you can do

There are two main ways in which you can help yourself, or your friends or family can help you. Firstly, try to get rid of any continuing life stresses, usually by making some social or behavioural changes in your life. Secondly, you can try various methods of countering the symptoms of depression.

It shouldn't be forgotten that voluntary agencies such as The Samaritans (see your local telephone directory) can play a very important role in helping you to help yourself.

Dealing with stresses

Depression is more common in people who have had to make major adjustments in their lives during the past six months to a year. These adjustments such as death of a family member, birth of a baby, loss of a job or moving house may result in continued stress, which can, over time, make you vulnerable to depression. So, in order to tackle the depression and prevent it creeping up on you again, it is important to resolve the stress.

Even happy events like getting married or having a baby can cause quite a bit of stress. Do remember this!

Priority tasks

The first priority in tackling stress is to ensure that you are getting enough exercise, nourishing diet and sleep. Alcohol, tobacco and non-prescribed drugs should be avoided, they are addictive and increase rather than relieve stress.

Exercise

There is only one way to keep the body trim and fit—by exercise. We all need some regular exercise, preferably daily. This might amount to no more than a pleasant, brisk 15 minute walk in the fresh air, but it could well be much more. At the very least you will be more likely to feel physically and mentally relaxed, to get a refreshing sleep, and your appetite will be stimulated. The important thing is that the exercise chosen should be pleasurable—which for some of us sloths is a problem!

Take things carefully

Whatever you decide to do in the way of exercise always bear the following points in mind:
- Warm up for two or three minutes before starting by stretching or running on the spot;
- Build up slowly and do not over-extend yourself—always exercise within the limits of comfort (let your breathing be your guide);
- If you feel excessively tired stop and rest, there is always tomorrow;
- When stopping exercise, cool down gradually and slowly to avoid stiffness;
- Exercise sessions three times a week for about 20 minutes, at a pace that keeps you moderately 'puffed' (not gasping for breath) are likely to be best for stimulating the muscles and circulation.

Diet

Eat a sensible diet to avoid the health hazards of being overweight and to reduce or prevent the risks of developing diseases known to be related to diet, such as heart disease, high blood pressure, bowel cancer, and late onset diabetes.

Less fat more fibre

The main principles are to eat far less fat and fatty foods, especially those containing saturated fats and cholesterols; increase dietary fibre by eating more whole grain cereals, pulses and fresh fruit and vegetables; and cut down on sugar and salt. This can be difficult as it goes against all that many of us hold dear such as the traditional Sunday lunch of roast beef, Yorkshire pudding, and roast potatoes! Don't go too quickly in your campaign for diet reform, change a few products at a time and add new foods rather than just cutting out those that you currently eat and are bad for you. If you 'live' for Sunday roast lunch don't abandon it completely; changing your diet should not be a torture, it should be fun!

Drink is important too

Be careful about what you drink. Too much tea or coffee can be overstimulating, and excessive alcohol is certainly no friend to good health.

Sleep

Getting enough good quality sleep can be a problem if you are depressed. Ways of improving sleep are on p. 57.

Some golden rules for reducing stress

Get your priorities right—sort out what really matters in your life;

Think ahead and try to anticipate how to get round difficulties;

Share your worries with family or friends whenever possible;

Stay sober, 'drowning your sorrows' will not help you;

Seek information, help and advice early, even though it takes an effort;

Try to develop a social network or circle of friends;

Take up hobbies and interests;

Exercise regularly;

Eat good, wholesome food;

Lead a regular lifestyle;

Give yourself treats and rewards for positive actions, attitudes and thoughts;

Don't regard difficulties as personal failings or failures—they are challenges to improve your ingenuity and stamina;

Don't be too hard on yourself—try to keep things in proportion;

Get to know yourself better—improve your defences and strengthen your weak points;

Don't 'bottle things up' or sit all night brooding—think realistically about problems and decide to take some appropriate action; if necessary distract yourself in some pleasant way;

Don't be reluctant to seek medical help if you are worried about your health;

Remember that there are many people who have faced similar circumstances and have dealt with them successfully, with or without the help of others;

There are always people who are willing and able to help, whatever the problem—don't be unwilling to benefit from their experience.

Countering the symptoms of depression

In addition to looking after yourself a problem-solving approach like the ones described below may help you define exactly what the stress is and devise a plan to cope with it. Although some stresses cannot be fully resolved in this way, you will usually find that your coping abilities improve so that the overall impact of stress is reduced.

Miserable feelings and unpleasant thoughts

Negative thoughts and feelings tend to focus your attention on things you don't like about yourself or your life. They tend to exaggerate problems so that they seem overwhelming and make you feel worse.

Although it may be difficult to distract yourself from unpleasant thoughts, it does help to decide not to think about them and fill your mind with something else. This can be done by a combination of:

- Concentrating on events around you such as other conversations, the number of blue things you can see...in fact anything that holds your attention;
- Any absorbing mental activity, such as mental arithmetic, games and puzzles, crosswords, reading—especially mental activities that you enjoy;

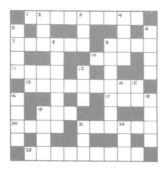

- Any physical activity that keeps you occupied, such as going for a walk, doing housework (well some people enjoy it) or taking a trip.

Think positive!

At the same time, unpleasant thoughts make you tend to underestimate your positive characteristics and ability to solve problems. A number of strategies may help you achieve a more balanced view of things:

- Make a list of your three best attributes—perhaps with the help of a friend or relative;
- Carry the list with you and read it to yourself three times whenever you find yourself thinking negative thoughts;
- Keep a daily diary or record of all the small pleasant events that happen and discuss these with a friend each day;
- Recall pleasant occasions in the past and plan pleasant ones for the future—this is best done in conversation with a friend;
- Avoid discussions about your unpleasant feelings—expressing unreasonable thoughts about yourself is unhelpful, tackling your real problems is helpful;
- Ask friends to interrupt such conversations politely and redirect your conversation to more positive ideas and more constructive suggestions;
- Always consider alternative explanations for unpleasant events or thoughts, don't always blame yourself first;
- Keep yourself and your mind occupied by planning and doing constructive tasks—avoid sitting or lying about daydreaming or doing nothing.

Anxiety, tension, worry or nervousness

Depression is almost always accompanied by symptoms of anxiety, tension, worry or nervousness, for example, muscle tension, trembling, cold sweats, 'butterflies' in the stomach, rapid or difficult and shallow breathing and rapid or irregular pounding heart beat. For many people, this response may be triggered off by seeing objects such as spiders or birds or by situations such as a closed space, a crowded supermarket, eating in a restaurant, or even meeting a friend. At other times, unpleasant thoughts, for example of dying or possible failure in work or relationships, may trigger off these feelings of anxiety and panic.

Find the trigger for panic

In almost all cases some situations or thoughts can be found to trigger off this panicky feeling. Once it occurs the feeling is so profound that most people want to escape from the situation that provoked it as quickly as possible, and wherever possible, to avoid any recurrence. Many people believe they are about to die of a heart attack, or that they are going mad and are about to lose control of themselves. Neither will occur: anxiety always goes away after a time. Panicky feelings are bodily sensations but they are not harmful.

Coping with panic

- Wait and the feelings will pass;
- Practise one of the plans below. Use it whenever you feel panicky;
- It can be helpful to start by taking a deep breath and then slowing down and deepening your breathing pattern;
- Try to distract your panicky thoughts, as described above, as this will stop you adding to the panic;
- As the panicky feelings subside, plan something pleasant to do next.

Plans for combatting anxiety

We all know that worrying is a pretty pointless activity—worrying never solved a problem. So here are three plans for countering worry and anxiety that you might find useful.

Plan A—problem solving

Put your worrying to a constructive purpose. Rather than endlessly pinpointing your problems, pick out one or two that seem really important and make specific plans to resolve them (you may find it helpful to do this with a friend). Sit down with a sheet of paper and a pencil and go through the following steps, making notes as you go:

- Write down exactly what the problem is;
- List five or six possible solutions to the problem—write down any ideas that occur to you, not merely 'good' ideas;
- Then weigh up the good and bad points of each idea in turn;
- Choose the solution that best fits your needs;
- Plan exactly the steps you would take to achieve the solution;
- Reassess your efforts after attempting to carry out your plan (remember to praise all your efforts);
- If you are unsuccessful, start again—this time trying a new plan.

Plan B—re-thinking an unpleasant experience

- List every feature of the experience: 'I'm sweating...the hairs on my arm are standing on end...my heart is pounding hard...I think I'm going to start screaming...my legs feel like jelly...I'm going to pass out' Write these down on a card;
- Talk yourself into staying with these unpleasant feelings. Tell yourself exactly how you feel, then remind yourself that the feelings will reach a peak and then get better;
- Re-label your experiences: imagine you are playing an energetic sport—the Cup Final, singles finals at Wimbledon—and that this accounts for your pounding heart, rapid breathing and feelings of excitement;
- Think catastrophic thoughts. Think of the worst possible thing that could happen to you, eg collapsing, screaming, throwing your clothes off, being incontinent. Plan exactly what you would do if it did actually happen.

Next time it will be a little easier to cope with the feelings, and with practice and monitoring you will find that you are beginning to control and overcome tension, worry and nervousness.

Plan C—relaxation

Relaxation is a most useful technique to practice when you feel tense or worried. There are a number of similar methods but one of the most widely used is described below. Read the instructions and familiarise yourself with them before having a go.

Do be patient and give yourself several tries before expecting the full beneficial results—for those of us who are very 'twitchy' it can take time to learn how to relax.

Keep a diary of your efforts, so that you can follow your progress day by day. A trusted friend or relative may help you to stick to the task, particularly when progress seems slow and difficult.

Preparation

Sit in a comfortable chair or (even better) lie down somewhere comfortable in a quiet, warm room where you will not be interrupted. If you are sitting, take off your shoes, uncross your legs, and rest your arms on the arms of the chair. If you are lying down, lie on your back with your arms at your sides. If necessary use a comfortable pillow for your head. Close your eyes and be aware of your body. Notice how you are breathing and where the muscular tensions are. Make sure you are comfortable.

Breathing

Start to breathe slowly and deeply, expanding your abdomen as you breathe in, then raising your rib cage to let more air in,

till your lungs are filled right to the top. Hold your breath for a couple of seconds and then breathe out slowly, allowing your rib cage and stomach to relax, and empty your lungs completely. Do not strain, with practice it will become much easier. Keep this slow, deep, rhythmic breathing going throughout your relaxation session.

Relaxing

After five to 10 minutes, when you have your breathing pattern established, start the following sequence tensing each part of the body on an in breath, holding your breath for 10 seconds while you keep your muscles tense; then relaxing and breathing out at the same time.

- Curl your toes hard and press your feet down;
- Press your heels down and bend your feet up;
- Tense your calf muscles;
- Tense your thigh muscles, straightening your knees and making your legs stiff;
- Make your buttocks tight;
- Tense your stomach as if to receive a punch;
- Bend your elbows and tense the muscles of your arms;
- Hunch your shoulders and press your head back into the cushion or pillow;
- Clench your jaws, frown, and screw up your eyes really tight;
- Tense all your muscles together.

Remember to breathe deeply, and be aware when you relax of the feeling of physical wellbeing and heaviness spreading through your body.

After you have finished the whole sequence and still breathing slowly and deeply, imagine something pleasant, for example a white rose on a black background, a beautiful country scene, a favourite painting. Try to 'see' the rose (or whatever) as clearly as possible, concentrating your attention on it for 30 seconds. Do not hold your breath during this time, continue to breathe as you have been doing. After this, go on to visualise another peaceful object of your choice in a similar fashion. Lastly, give yourself the instruction that when you open your eyes you will be perfectly relaxed but alert.

Short routine

When you have become familiar with this technique, if you want to relax at any time when you have only a few minutes, do the sequence in shortened form, leaving out some muscle groups, but always working from your feet upwards. For example, you might do numbers 1, 4, 6, 8 and 10 if you do not have time to do the whole sequence.

Coping with sleep disturbance

Difficulties with sleep affect almost everyone from time to time, but sleep problems are particularly troublesome for people with depression. These can take the following forms:
- Difficulty getting to sleep even when tired;
- Waking up much earlier than usual and not being able to get back to sleep;
- Restless sleep with repeated waking during the night;
- Excessive sleep during the day.

How much sleep do I need?

Sleep requirements vary greatly from person to person and from time to time. The commonest cause of disturbed sleep patterns is being worried about not getting eight hours sleep, but not everybody needs this amount each night. As we grow older, for example, we often need no more than four or five hours sleep. The older we get the longer it takes to get off to sleep, the more frequently we wake during the night, and the less total sleep we have. The amount of sleep we need also depends on the physical activity we undertake and our state of health. When we are ill, considerably more than eight hours sleep may be needed in any 24 hour period.

Quality not quantity

The quality of sleep is more important than the quantity. A few hours of relaxed, natural sleep may be more invigorating than many hours of drug-induced sleep.

What causes disturbed sleep?

In depression, persistent worrying leads to difficulties in relaxing and may lead to sleep difficulties, especially getting off to sleep. Early morning wakening is typical of more serious depression. Other causes include:
- Stimulants—sleeping difficulty is often caused by a high intake of caffeine in tea and coffee, as well as in cola drinks and nicotine in cigarettes;
- Rebound effects of sedative drugs—many sedative drugs that induce sleep tend to act as stimulants when their sedative effects wear off. This effect may be caused by sleeping tablets. Alcohol has a similar effect. This results in

getting off to sleep quickly, but waking up within a few hours with difficulty getting back to sleep;

- Changing activity schedules—people who do shift work may find it difficult to adjust to changing sleep and activity patterns. Similar problems may arise on holiday, especially when long distance travel and changes of climate are involved;
- Physical illness—pain is a common cause of disturbed sleep. Breathing difficulties, a chronic cough, or the need to pass water frequently may also interrupt sleep.

Coping with disturbed sleep

To begin with, it is helpful to make a daily diary or record of your sleep pattern. This will allow you to see whether the problem is as bad as you think and whether it is getting worse, better or staying much the same over a period of time. It will also help you to judge whether anything you have tried to improve your sleep has had the desired effect.

Record the times you sleep in each 24 hour period. Record the quality of each sleep, eg is it restful, fitful or dozing? Note whether the sleep was in bed, in a chair or in front of the television. Finally, note whether you used anything to help you sleep (drug, hot drink, relaxation, etc). All those cat naps in an armchair, in front of the television and on the train can make up for sleep lost during the night.

Hints on getting to sleep

- Try not to worry about the amount of sleep you have, this only makes things worse;
- Go to bed at your regular time;
- If you find that you have been going to bed too early, go to bed a quarter of an hour later each evening for a week or so until your sleep improves;
- If you wake tired in the morning try bringing your bedtime forward a quarter to half an hour each night until you wake refreshed and not too early;
- Avoid sleeping during the day so that you are more tired at bedtime;
- Try eating your evening meal at a regular time, several hours before you go to bed;
- Take some regular exercise. A quiet stroll in the evening will help you relax and make you feel more tired. But avoid stimulating exercise before bedtime;
- Avoid stimulating drinks and tobacco close to bedtime. Reduce your intake of tea, coffee, or cola to no more than two to three drinks daily, and have your last drink several hours before bedtime;
- A warm milky drink before bed helps you relax and will stop any hunger pangs;
- A warm bath may also help you to relax before bed;
- A regular routine at bedtime helps you get into the frame of mind for sleep;
- Don't listen to the radio or read in bed unless you have found that these are particularly useful ways of helping you relax;
- Avoid sedative drugs (unless specially prescribed by your doctor) and alcohol at bedtime;
- Try the relaxation technique (described above) while lying comfortably in bed;
- If you are unable to sleep because you are worrying and cannot put your problems out of your mind:
    - get up
    - take a piece of paper and pen
    - write down exactly what the problem is
    - write a list of every possible solution to the problem (good ideas as well as bad ones)
    - choose a solution that you can begin the next day
    - plan exactly how you would carry out the plan.
- Don't lie awake for longer than 30 minutes. If you cannot sleep, get up and find a constructive activity.

Countering loss of interest, slowed activity, lack of energy

- Set some goals for your daily activities—eg I will get up by..., go to meet a friend..., read an article in the newspaper;
- In small steps, structure a full programme of constructive activities for the day;
- Pinpoint small areas of interest that you can easily perform and build upon them;
- Avoid comparing your current levels of performance and interest with those in the past—concentrate on the 'here and now' and on the future;
- If a task seems too difficult don't despair, break it down into even easier steps and start again more slowly;
- Above all, *reward yourself for your efforts*;
- Try to have others around you to encourage and praise you for every small step you take.

Loss of appetite

- Eat small portions of food that you particularly like;
- Take your time eating;
- Temporarily avoid situations that make you feel under pressure to finish eating;
- Drink plenty of fluids, especially fruit juices and milk;
- Weight loss may be an important indicator of the extent of depression, so if you begin to lose weight, seek professional help from your GP.

Loss of sexual drive

- Decreased interest in sex is frequently a feature of depressive illness and is a cause of much distress;
- Enjoy those aspects of your sexual relationship that are still a pleasure;
- Explain to your partner that your loss of interest and affection is a temporary symptom of your condition, not a rejection of him or her;
- Treating depression does not always restore your libido. Discuss problems early with your GP, another professional adviser or confidant.

Loss of confidence and avoidance of depressing situations

Both loss of confidence and avoidance of depressing situations can be overcome by facing difficulties gradually. The aim is to face up to difficult situations in easy stages, building up confidence to try more difficult situations by using graded practice.

Defining the problem

The first step is to ask:
- Which situations do I avoid?
- What tasks do I put off because of the strain they cause?
- What problems do I avoid thinking about?

Make a list

The next step is to make a list of the things you avoid, put off, or try not to think about:

- Arrange these in their order of increasing difficulty for you to face up to;
- Take the first item on the list as your first target to practice thinking about or facing up to. Describe the target you are aiming for very clearly in writing;
- Practice thinking about it or facing up to it as often as possible until it is no longer a difficulty. An hour a day, either in one session or in a number of shortened sessions might be appropriate for most targets. If something seems too difficult, break it down into smaller practice steps or shorter practice periods and gradually build up the practice time;
- Move on to the next item and repeat the process.
- Do not be put off if you feel a bit worse to begin with, as this is almost inevitable;
- Be prepared to put some effort into regaining your confidence.

Practice regularly, frequently, and for fairly long periods—depending on the nature of the task.

'Try to face your Dragons'

Get someone else to help

It is common to think that you are not making any progress to begin with, and to underrate your achievements. Therefore it is helpful to have a member of the family or a friend to give you an independent opinion about progress and to give you encouragement.

> Remember to praise all your successes, give yourself a pat on the back and promise yourself a treat when you have achieved a previously stated target.

Setbacks

Everyone has setbacks from day to day. These are to be expected, and you should try to keep your mind on your long term goals.
- Try to approach the problem in a different way;
- Try to approach the difficulty in smaller steps or stages;

61

- Try to continue your practice because eventually this will help you overcome your difficulties;
- Remember that you will probably be more successful if you can make your activities or rewards as enjoyable as possible.

Remember your good points and remind yourself of them regularly

Making a note of improvements

A simple daily or weekly record or diary will help you keep track on improvement. The first signs are usually quite small, sometimes hardly noticeable. A diary will help you see exactly what happened—you shouldn't rely on memory as this can be very far off the mark. Also, people have a tendency to remember setbacks more than successes. Again, it is helpful to involve someone else in assessing your improvement, to give an independent opinion.

The message is, write down what happened

- Score yourself from 1 (bad) to 10 (good) for each day or week;
- Write down all your successes, large or small;
- Write down what self-help technique you were using, what target you were trying to achieve, and whether you were practising it regularly;
- Write down what you did not avoid thinking about or doing;
- Write down what you did for enjoyment or fun;
- Look back at your diary every week to see what progress you have made and to make plans for what you intend to achieve the next week.

7 Professional help

There are three main types of professional help available for people suffering from depressive illness: medical, psychological, and social treatments. In practice, however, these elements are often combined in the various treatments offered by different professionals—except that prescriptions for drugs can only be written by doctors.

General practitioners, social workers, clinical psychologists, community psychiatric nurses, counsellors and psychiatrists have important roles to play in the treatment of people with depressive illness. Common to all their approaches, and at least as important as the specific features of treatment, are the general characteristics these people display—such as acceptance, warmth, genuineness, empathy, a tolerant attitude, dependability, continuity and an interest that allows them to take even seemingly minor problems seriously.

Your family doctor

For most people with depression, particularly those with few or no confidants, the family doctor becomes the first and chief source of help. Doctors deal with all aspects of life that affect health, but like other people they vary in their response to people with depressive illnesses.

One difficulty is that doctors may not always recognise depression if your main complaint is of a physical symptom—even though the symptom is really part and parcel of a depressive illness. Another problem is that many of us are reluctant to admit to ourselves, or anyone else, that we are emotionally depressed.

Recognising depressive illness can be difficult for both patients and doctors. If, however, you think that depression is at the root of your troubles, think out clearly what you are going to say to the doctor about your symptoms and feelings before you go to see him or her. If necessary, write it all down so that you make yourself as clear as possible.

Early action

Since depressive illness causes changes in body chemistry and functioning as well as the heightened experience of life stress, it is best treated by a combination of medical and social methods. In addition, any physical illness present needs to be treated thoroughly.

Stay at work if you can

People suffering from depression who are still at work usually do not need to stop work or to break social links, indeed it is usually an advantage to keep occupied in these ways as they can help to maintain your self esteem.

A good night's sleep

The doctor's first step is to ensure that you get a good night's sleep. If necessary he may prescribe an antidepressant drug with sedative properties. Sometimes this will make you feel very 'dopey' for the first few nights, but it is usually best to start with a high dose and then reduce gradually if necessary.

Anxiety

Daytime restlessness or tension may also be a target of antidepressant treatment, though the doctor will aim to achieve relaxation without drowsiness. These measures alone may lead to a general lifting of depression.

Help from others

Depressed people often feel lonely, and an attempt may be made by your doctor to muster the concern of family and friends as this often proves helpful. Your doctor may also suggest a temporary change of environment, such as going to stay with a friend or having a short holiday, as this may also bring some relief.

Hospital treatment

For more seriously ill people, admission to hospital may have to be considered, particularly if there is a risk of suicide, of harm being caused to others, of antisocial behaviour, or if the home environment is specially unhelpful. When necessary, compulsory admission to hospital can be life-saving.

Points to remember

- Acute depression precipitated by life events and mild depression may improve within a few days of early medical treatment;
- Some people stay well simply with refreshing sleep and daytime sedation;
- If the depression does not lift, or if any improvement is only temporary (seven to 14 days), more specific medical treatment of depression is likely to be required.

Specific medical treatments

The main medical treatments for depressive illness are antidepressant drugs and electroconvulsive therapy (ECT). Drug treatment is far more common than ECT, which, though equally effective, is usually reserved for a small minority of the most seriously ill people, who are at strong risk of suicide or whose depression is life threatening. Psychosurgery is very rarely used nowadays and is performed only in severely ill people with long standing depression, when it sometimes provides welcome relief.

Not enough

No patient is adequately treated with *antidepressant drugs* alone. *Counselling* may be particularly useful if your depression seems to arise from the persisting effects of an unsatisfactory childhood. An unrewarding life style suggests the need for *social and behavioural changes* and if your view of yourself and life is negative, a *cognitive approach* may be helpful. I will look at psychological and social treatments in later chapters but let us first consider medical treatments in greater detail.

8 Medical treatment

Antidepressant drugs are particularly indicated where your doctor diagnoses moderate to severe depression and if you have symptoms like the following:

- Sleep disturbance;
- Loss of appetite;
- Loss of weight;
- Loss of interest in sex;
- Loss of interests and hobbies;
- Inactivity;
- Fatigue;
- Marked anxiety;
- Impaired concentration;
- Suicidal thoughts.

The presence of some or many of these symptoms and persistently low mood is a useful measure of your psychobiological response and helps to determine whether your illness is 'reactive'/'neurotic' or 'endogenous'/'manic-depressive' in origin. The more noticeable your physical symptoms, the more likely it is that medical treatment such as antidepressant drugs will be successful. But remember that antidepressants act upon depressive symptoms, they can do little to help an unhappy development, an unrewarding life style, or negative thinking.

Life stress and antidepressants

The presence of life stress is of little relevance to the use of antidepressants. It is not the stress itself but your psychobiological response to it that is important in the choice of drug treatment. It is better to ignore presumed causes of depression and concentrate on the pattern of symptoms.

How do antidepressants work?

The theory is that these drugs increase the levels of certain chemical transmitters (called monoamines) in the brain, which are usually reduced in people with depression. Although the effect of antidepressants on the transmitters is rapid, for unknown reasons changes take about two weeks to produce an improvement in the symptoms of depression.

What effects do antidepressants have?

Most people experience some relief from the symptoms of depression after taking antidepressant drugs and although there are many different brands, they all work in a similar way. In the first few days, antidepressants help most with sleep and tend to have a calming effect, sometimes making you feel more lethargic. This effect, however, gives way to increasing alertness and energy after a week or two of taking the medicine regularly. It is very important to recognise that it may take four to six weeks before the maximum benefits of antidepressant medication is noticed.

Your doctor will usually give you a limited supply of drugs at first. Some people with suicidal tendencies feel so low that they haven't even the 'strength' to kill themselves. The danger time for them is when they are becoming more active. Doctors are aware of this possibility and will not therefore provide the means of suicide by giving too many pills.

Things you should know about antidepressants

- Do not expect immediate benefits from antidepressants;
- Antidepressant treatment will usually continue until symptoms disappear;
- Most depressions lift within three months to a year;
- Some patients seem to benefit from antidepressant treatment at half dose for several months to prevent relapse;
- After a month of wellbeing, your drug dose may slowly be reduced, continuing for one to two weeks at each new dose level and watching lest symptoms reappear, as they are likely to if you stop or reduce too soon;
- Antidepressant treatment should usually be reduced when your social circumstances are stable;
- Antidepressant treatment should not usually be reduced if special life stresses arise.

Side effects of antidepressant drugs

The side effects of antidepressants are unavoidable and affect most people to some extent. They tend to be worst in the first few days of starting or of increasing the dose, but they are usually mild and reversible. Older people may be especially sensitive to side effects, especially dizziness and fainting.

The following side effects may occur within a day of starting antidepressant drugs, and most will respond to a reduced dose or change of medication:

- Dry mouth;
- Slight blurring of vision;
- Dizziness or faintness on standing or changing position quickly;
- Sweating;
- Constipation;
- Headache;
- Difficulty passing water;
- Some antidepressants cause sedation, drowsiness and un-steadiness—for example, amitriptyline;
- Others cause people to be more alert—for example, nortriptyline.

Later side effects (after two or more weeks) will also usually improve with a reduced dose or change of drug, and include:

- Tremors;
- Gain in weight;
- Disturbed sexual function.

Antidepressants and alcohol

It is also important to know that alcohol increases the side effects of antidepressants, and so these will be much more likely to occur if you drink alcohol while taking antidepressants.

Antidepressants and other illnesses

Finally, people with certain medical conditions or on certain drugs are particularly susceptible to side effects, these include:

- Conditions causing difficulty in passing water;
- Glaucoma (an eye complaint);
- Conditions causing heart irregularities;
- Epilepsy;
- High blood pressure.

Report side effects

It is wise to make a note of any side effects and to report them to your doctor, who will advise you what to do. He may, for example, advise you to take the antidepressant at bedtime so that you are asleep when you might otherwise be troubled by side effects, or change the prescription to an antidepressant without the particular side effect complained of.

First choice antidepressant drugs

Antidepressant drugs of first choice are usually tricyclic (or related) antidepressants. They are called 'tricyclic' because of their chemical structure, which consists of three (or more) rings. Different people's bodies handle these drugs in different ways and for this reason there is quite a wide range in response and sensitivity to different doses. The two longest established and best known tricyclic antidepressants are:
- Amitriptyline (sedative—agitated and anxious patients benefit);
- Imipramine (less sedative—withdrawn and apathetic patients benefit).

How long should antidepressant treatment continue?

It can take up to six weeks for significant improvement to occur in patients with moderate to severe depression treated with antidepressant drugs. To prevent relapse of the current episode treatment of a moderate to severe depression should probably continue for at least four months after initial recovery.

Main side effects of tricyclic antidepressants

- dry mouth;
- blurred vision;
- constipation;
- difficulty passing urine;
- rapid heart beat;
- drowsiness;
- confusion;
- postural dizziness;
- sedation;
- tremor;
- sweating;
- weight gain.

When is an alternative tricyclic antidepressant used?

If a first choice antidepressant doesn't suit you because of undesirable side effects or because it does not work well for you, or if you have a medical illness incompatible with the drug, there are a large number of other tricyclic or related antidepressant drugs that may be used as an alternative.

Some other tricyclic (or related) antidepressants

Drugs with more sedative effects include:
- Dothiepin;
- Doxepin;
- Maprotiline;
- Mianserin;
- Trazodone;
- Trimipramine.

Drugs with less sedative effects include:
- Butriptyline;
- Clomipramine;
- Desipramine;
- Imipramine;
- Iprindole;
- Lofepramine;
- Nortriptyline;
- Viloxazine.

Drugs with some stimulant action include:
- Protriptyline.

Lack of response to tricyclic antidepressant drugs

Up to a third of people with severe depressive illnesses either fail to respond or respond only partially to treatment with tricyclic antidepressants. When this happens, specific psychological or social treatment may be required. For many, other types of antidepressant may be tried, either alone or in combination with one or other of the tricyclic antidepressants mentioned above. Combination treatment can be dangerous, however, because some of these drugs interact badly with each other, and for this reason it is best left to specialists.

Other drugs used to treat depression

The chief examples of other drugs used to treat depression are:
- Monoamine oxidase inhibitors (MAOIs);
- Flupenthixol (in low doses);
- Tryptophan;
- Lithium.

Monoamine oxidase inhibitors (MAOIs)

These drugs are not often prescribed because they can react with some foods and other drugs to cause serious side effects.

The main examples of MAOIs are:

- Phenalzine;
- Isocarboxazid;
- Tranylcypromine (most hazardous because of stimulant action).

Depressed patients with anxieties, phobias, and bodily symptoms, and those who have failed to respond to tricyclic or related antidepressants sometimes respond well to MAOIs.

What you should know about MAOIs

Response to MAOIs may take three weeks or more to become apparent, so it is necessary to give them a trial lasting about four to six weeks before concluding that they are ineffective.

Certain drugs and tyramine-containing foods cause an interaction with MAOIs leading to a dangerous rise in blood pressure—an early warning of which is a throbbing headache. This interaction lasts for up to 14 days after treatment with MAOIs has stopped so tricyclic and related antidepressants should not be taken for at least 14 days.

Don't eat cheese, pickled herring or broad bean pods if you are taking MAOIs

Points to remember about MAOIs

While taking MAOIs and up to 14 days after stopping this treatment:
- Do not eat cheese, pickled herring, or broad bean pods;
- Do not eat or drink bovril, oxo, marmite, or a similar meat or yeast extract;
- Eat only fresh foods—avoid game and food that could be stale or 'going off', especially meat, fish, poultry or offal;
- Do not take any other medicines (including treatment for coughs and colds, pain relievers, tonics and laxatives) without consulting your doctor or pharmacist (if these drugs are purchased over the counter);
- Avoid alcohol;
- Record and report any unusual or severe symptoms to your doctor.

Side effects of MAOIs

Side effects of MAOIs include:
- Dizziness;
- Insomnia;
- Increased appetite;
- Agitated feeling;
- Otherwise similar to other antidepressants, as noted above.

Other drugs occasionally used to treat depression

Various other drugs may be useful for some of the symptoms of depression. Tranquillisers such as diazepam or thioridazine are sometimes given, particularly if worry and agitation are severe. Unfortunately these drugs may slow down thinking and further reduce energy levels and are therefore probably best used only in exceptional cases.

Long term treatment

Patients with frequent recurrences of depressive illness or chronic depression are sometimes maintained on antidepressants for periods of several years in an effort to prevent or 'damp down' future episodes. This seems to be a safe procedure if undertaken under medical supervision. However, regular consideration should always be given to the question of the continuing need for long term antidepressant medication.

Lithium

Lithium salts are sometimes used to prevent or limit depressive illnesses, as well as to treat manic episodes. Lithium treatment is only given to carefully selected people and is usually only carried out under specialist guidance. Since lithium is prescribed for relatively long periods (three to five years initially, and sometimes 'for life') the likelihood of recurrences of depression has to be weighed against the risks and side effects of the treatment. These are greater than usual and require very careful monitoring, including regular blood tests and medical examinations to ensure that the level of lithium in the blood is stable within a narrow range.

Side effects

The main side effects of lithium tend to be caused by high levels of lithium in the blood, sometimes aggravated by the use of water pills or dehydration. The signs of lithium toxicity are progressive and include:
- Tremor;
- Blurred vision;
- Passing excess urine;
- Thirst, leading to drinking a lot of fluid;
- Anorexia, vomiting, diarrhoea;
- Mild drowsiness and sluggishness;
- Giddiness and incoordination;
- Slurring;
- Eye problems;
- Kidney problems;
- Fits.

Most of these side effects are reversed when the dose is reduced or temporarily stopped. It is important to ask the doctor for advice if these side effects persist or seem to be getting worse, as eventually you can lose consciousness if no action is taken to reduce the blood lithium level.

Long term problems

Long term use of lithium may be associated with changes in kidney tissue and function, and thyroid, skin and heart problems. These are other important reasons why the decision to use lithium has to be weighed up carefully beside the severity of the depressive illness and the potential it may have for disrupting the patient's life and work.

Electroconvulsive therapy (ECT)

This is mainly used to treat people with severe and life threatening depressive illnesses, particularly those who have stopped eating and drinking because of their illness, those with delusions and people with strong suicidal ideas and urges. In all of these circumstances a quick and sure response is required. Electroconvulsive therapy is usually also considered for people who remain severely depressed after antidepressant drug treatment and other methods have failed to help them.

What is ECT?

Electroconvulsive therapy involves having a small current of electricity passed through the brain via both temples (bilateral ECT) or via one temple (unilateral ECT), while the patient is unconscious under a general anaesthetic. The treatment is usually carried out for people who are already in hospital, but occasionally ECT is given to people as outpatients. Although the procedure is safe, painless and without many side effects, it has a frightening and off-putting reputation.

How does it work?

Electroconvulsive therapy causes the patient to have a mild convulsion. It is not clear exactly how it works, but it is thought to influence the chemical transmitter systems in the brain, like antidepressants do.

Within a few minutes of ECT the anaesthetic wears off and the patient comes round. Sometimes there is mild confusion, headache, stiff muscles, or nausea for an hour or so but with rest these pass off uneventfully.

Why give ECT?

It is the quickest treatment for more severe types of depressive illness, and patients receiving ECT begin to show improvement within days or a week or so of starting. The treatment is given as a course, often of six ECTs at a rate of two per week. Some people benefit from longer courses or from more frequent applications, it depends on individual circumstances and responses.

Electroconvulsive therapy is safe in the frail, the elderly, those with high blood pressure, those with Parkinson's disease, people with heart problems and stroke (from about three months after an attack) and in pregnancy, and the general risks are equivalent to those involved in having a general anaesthetic for other reasons.

Unwanted side effects

One of the commonest complaints made of ECT is that it causes memory impairment—for example, difficulty in remembering names or learning new information. This is particularly likely in older people with depression and a dementing illness. In fact, although a great deal of research has been done in trying to find out exactly what the memory problems are, the studies have produced conflicting results and there is no definite evidence that ECT causes memory disturbance. In any case, complaints are made less frequently of unilateral ECT, which is usually given on the right temple to avoid affecting the speech centre of the brain, disturbance of which is thought to be responsible for confusion and memory complaints. Memory difficulties, when they arise, are usually short lived, disappearing within a few weeks of stopping treatment.

Can you refuse ECT?

Finally, in common with all treatments, the patient has the right to refuse consent for ECT. With drugs, if you accept a prescription you are deemed to be consenting to treatment. In the case of ECT, however, you would be asked to sign a consent form before the treatment could be given.

9 Psychological treatment

The traditional medical approach to the treatment of mental illness has been criticised for being too narrow and neglecting personal and social aspects. Because of this criticism a variety of psychological approaches have been developed to treat depression, either in addition to medical treatment or alone, and particularly in the treatment of milder depression. Psychological treatments may prove to be of value in mild to moderate depressive illnesses and may also have a beneficial role in the long term treatment of those with severe depressive illnesses.

Basis of psychotherapy

Any treatment for depression that does not use drugs or other physical methods could be called psychotherapy. The most important part of psychotherapy is talking, and it is the ideas behind the therapy, the way it is applied and the nature of the relationships that take place between patients and therapists that differentiate the various types of psychotherapy.

Schools of thought

Many depressed patients seem unable to express anger or hostility at first. One psychotherapeutic view of depression is that it is the inward turning of the aggressive instinct. Some schools of therapy emphasise the importance of loss (of loved ones, objects, or cherished ideas) in depression, drawing attention to the similarities between mourning and melancholia. Others propose that we humans have an inborn tendency to seek attachments with others that lead to reciprocal, personal, social bonds (attachment bonds) and to experiences of warmth, nurture and protection. Disruption of these bonds may make people vulnerable to depression.

Attachment bonds

Depending on the approach taken by your psychotherapist, you may be helped to express and redirect your anger and hostility at more appropriate outside objects or you may work together to examine current personal relationships and to understand how they have developed from experiences with attachment figures in childhood, adolescence and adulthood. The concept of attachment bonds provides a basis for understanding the personal background of depression and for developing strategies to correct distortions produced by faulty or inadequate attachments in childhood.

Evidence to support the importance of interpersonal and social bonds comes from the observation that people with depression tend to have fewer good friends and fewer contacts outside the household. Strong attachment bonds seem to be especially important and valuable when people are faced with adversity and stress.

Psychotherapy and relationships

The psychotherapeutic approach to the treatment of depression has arisen out of these kind of theories. It views disturbances in personal relationships as a cause of depression and assumes that depressed mood arises from relationship difficulties such as:
- Loss;
- Disputes about roles (especially the roles of husband and wife);
- Role transitions (becoming a mother, divorce);
- Lack of close relationships.

Psychotherapists therefore focus on:
- Current and past relationships with important people, such as family and friends;
- The quality and pattern of these relationships, with regard to:
  * dealing with authority figures
  * dealing with dominance and submission
  * dependence and autonomy
  * intimacy, trust and sexual relationships
- Your responses to separation and losses.

In essence, psychotherapeutic treatment is concerned with identifying problems in your closest relationships and in considering alternative ways of behaving and thinking.

So what do you talk about?

The discussions between patient and therapist concentrate on:
- Emotions generated by close relationships (including warmth, anger, trust, envy, jealousy);
- Family relationships;
- Friendship;
- Work;
- Attitudes to neighbourhood and community.

Any disadvantages

Many people assume that one or other variety of psycho-therapy would suit them. Psychotherapy, especially psycho-analysis, which may take years, is often prolonged, intensive, and expensive. In addition, it is not easily available throughout the country. And it is very difficult to judge its benefits. This applies to psychotherapy given individually or in groups. For these reasons, and because it is possible for some people to feel worse and more stressed after psychotherapy, this treatment is generally considered inappropriate for most people with depressive illness.

79

Support and counselling

General practitioners and most health professionals often find themselves in the position of giving emotional support, advice and counselling to depressed patients in an effort to provide reassurance, encouragement and sympathy. Indeed, this is probably the commonest and most successful treatment for most people with mild and moderate depressive illnesses. In many cases, listening may be more important than giving advice—provided that listening means not only hearing the words spoken, but also attending to what the patient is saying and trying to understand how she or he feels.

Important factors in support and counselling

Support and counselling:

- Allow you to express appropriate emotions and give you reassurance about the normality of these emotions; a hand on the shoulder may do more good than any number of words;
- Any irrational anger and guilt is accepted by others and not discounted;
- You can talk through events leading up to the crisis;
- You can test the reality of events described;
- You can explore the implications;
- You may be given encouragement to seek new directions in life.

But beware of seeing problems as entirely due to illness and beware of becoming dependent on professional helpers.

Don't forget that you can get a great deal of support and counselling from ministers of religion and voluntary bodies, most notably The Samaritans. The British Association for Counselling, 37A Sheep Street, Rugby, Warwicks CV1 3AD, will be able to help find local counsellors.

Cognitive therapy

Cognitive therapy is a relatively new form of psychological treatment which proposes that a negative way of thinking is the basis of depressive moods. Hopelessness and helplessness are central features of depression and reflect what therapists call the 'cognitive triad'—a negative view of yourself, negative interpretations of your experiences and a negative view of the future.

Theory

According to cognitive theory there are two types of abnormality in depression. Firstly, intrusive thoughts concerned with low self regard, self criticism and self blame are common. Secondly, distortions in thinking and understanding are also present ('cognitive distortions') which bias the person's view of reality and makes it possible for him or her to believe in the ideas represented in the intrusive thoughts.

Cognitive distortions

Four kinds of cognitive distortions are described:
- Forming an interpretation when there are no facts to support the conclusions or when the conclusion is contrary to evidence;
- Focusing on a detail taken out of context and ignoring other important features;
- Drawing general conclusions on the basis of a single incident;
- Errors of magnification or minimisation in evaluating situations.

Aims of cognitive therapy

The cognitive approach centres on the notion that the way we think affects our emotions and behaviour. This explanation of depression can be contrasted with the traditional view which regards faulty thinking as a *symptom* of depression rather than it's *cause*. The mood swings that are a typical feature of depression are brought on by the person's own thoughts. These take the form of negative ideas concerning the person in relation to his environment which have been rehearsed and reinforced over a number of years so that they become automatic. As with many bad habits, the individual is generally unaware that he is doing this. The principle aims of cognitive therapy are to help the patient to recognise his unhelpful automatic thoughts and replace them with a more flexible and adaptive way of thinking.

Therapy in practice

Cognitive techniques used in the treatment of depressive disorders aim to alter maladaptive thinking by explanation, discussion and questioning of assumptions.

Recurrent intrusive thoughts

Recurrent intrusive thoughts that increase your depressed mood are identified by getting you to keep written records of moods and thinking in everyday life.

Negative thinking

Counterbalancing negative thinking is achieved by getting you to examine the evidence for and against these wrong and negative ideas and in doing so to become aware of and correct the logical errors which allowed you to arrive at and sustain these ideas and beliefs. The aim is to help you to challenge the underlying assumptions and to find appropriate alternative ideas.

Solving problems helps

Problem solving helps you to work out solutions to persistent life problems that are maintaining your depression. The therapist will assist you to:
- Define the problem;
- Divide it into manageable parts;
- Think of alternative solutions;
- Select the best solution;
- Carry it out and examine the result.

Changing behaviour

Your therapist may help you choose actions which are likely to change negative ways of thinking—'learning from experience'. Some therapists recommend methods of increasing your assertiveness; others use 'pleasant event therapy', which focuses on increasing your pleasant and rewarding experiences; and others employ 'self control therapy', which emphasises self monitoring, self evaluation and self reinforcement to correct problems with self control in coping with negative experiences.

Back to basics

If you distort the evidence in one or more of these ways, your 'automatic' depressive thoughts are likely to be unrealistic and maladaptive. It is not enough simply to help you change the content of a particular thought, it is essential that you should recognise and change the reasoning process which led you to a false conclusion if you are to avoid making similar errors in the future. Although the cognitive therapist pays particular attention to the 'automatic' thoughts which precede a change of mood, he or she is also concerned to question the deeper assumptions someone makes about the world, since deeper assumptions give power to the 'automatic' thoughts.

Gaining insight
The first task is to help you become aware of any negative thinking and to recognise the relationship between it and depressive changes of mood. This can be done by helping you to recognise 'automatic' thoughts during treatment, when the depressive episode can be relived using role play.

Objectivity
A second task is to help you to develop different ways of interpreting events. For example, you may be encouraged to stand back from a problem in order to get a more objective view of it. Different ideas may be sought and you may be asked to rate their correctness. Once you are able to think of alternative ways of interpreting events you may be asked to keep a daily record of mood changes and the thoughts associated with them. You may be asked to reason with 'automatic' thoughts and suggest other possible interpretations to yourself as soon as a lowering of mood becomes apparent.

Inquiring
The third phase of the process is to encourage you to test out the beliefs and attitudes associated with depression in a systematic way. Instead of treating ideas as fact, you will be helped to see that it is possible to discover the truth or otherwise of your beliefs through inquiry.

Change is needed

Treatment progressively prepares people for change, but usually a change in behaviour is required before most are willing to discard a false belief altogether. One way to bring this about is for the therapist and patient to identify a relevant task which the patient can carry out as 'homework'.

Breaking barriers

As you improve and learn the cognitive approach, the focus of treatment moves to the deeper assumptions which are thought to underly your depressive thinking. Unless these are identified and modified you are likely to become depressed again in the future. Since these beliefs have usually been present from an early age they are highly resistent to change. There are no simple techniques for eliciting these faulty assumptions but a useful start is for you to identify recurring depressive themes in your life. The best way to break the pattern is to encourage you to act against these deeper assumptions.

How long does this take?

Approximately 15 sessions over three months are sufficient for most people. Two sessions a week are usually held in the first month followed by weekly meetings thereafter.

10 Social treatment

For the sociologist, depression is the result of a social structure that deprives some people from control over their destiny. This view focuses on factors such as urbanisation, the influence of social class, racial membership, ethnic background and political and economic forces in causing depression and provides an explanation for increased rates of mental illness among certain groups. For example, a feminist interpretation of the high rates of depression in women would be that women are oppressed and that depressive feelings of helplessness and worthlessness reflect womens' current status in society.

Practical points

In practical terms, social treatment covers all efforts to improve a patient's wellbeing by changing aspects of his or her social life, particularly in regard to family relationships, work and leisure activities. Of course, defined in this way, virtually all treatment consists of some social elements—even visiting the GP is a social event!

At the most simple level, having a holiday, taking time off work, or taking up a new interest are all important social means of trying to relieve depression. Family and voluntary social support can take the form of visiting or befriending depressed people. This can bring relief through the presence of a sympathetic ear and a shoulder to cry on. Education and religion both offer great opportunities for social sustenance to people suffering from depressive illness.

Family therapy

More complicated forms of treatment also contain a strong social ingredient. Family approaches to treatment, sometimes called 'family therapy', treat the person with depression in relation to their family. This does not mean that the family is held responsible for the individual's depression but it is clear that many of the problems of depression revolve around difficulties in the way family members communicate and relate to each other. Bringing the family together for group discussions is sometimes a powerful way of helping everyone pull together instead of apart, of improving communication and of helping parents develop better relationships with their children and vice versa.

Group therapy

Group therapy is allied to this approach. Discussing problems in a group helps combat social isolation, reinforces for people with depression that they are not alone in the symptoms they are suffering and provides the opportunity for mutual encouragement and discussion of practical ways of overcoming depression.

Occupational therapy, art therapy, play therapy, dance therapy, movement therapy, drama therapy, music therapy, physiotherapy and gymnastics all help people develop new social skills as well as practise old ones, increasing self confidence and self sufficiency. All aim to provide enjoyment, diversion, stimulation and increased self esteem and achievement in a social context.

11 Which treatment is best?

As I pointed out earlier, elements of the three main types of professional help available—medical, psychological and social—are often combined in the various treatment 'packages' offered by different professionals. While the more severe forms of depressive illness often respond best to medical treatment, this is not always the case. About a third of more seriously ill people are not helped by antidepressant drugs and approximately another third find it difficult to stick with their course of drugs—for one reason or another. Unfortunately, the full choice of psychological and social treatments is not available everywhere, which means that you may not be able to get the sort of treatment you want.

The best is the one that works

I cannot be more specific than to say that the best treatment is the one that works for you. All methods I have discussed are found helpful for some people, and if one does not seem to be working after a fair trial, you should try another until your depression lifts. As we have already seen, the variety of psychological and social therapies can be quite confusing, so, as an aide memoire, I have listed the main ones in the Table below.

Types of social and psychotherapy available

Psychotherapy
- Any form of treatment that does not use physical methods like drugs may be called psychotherapy, and so there are a large number of psychotherapies;

- Talking is the main tool of treatment, and the different schools encourage talking about different aspects of your condition;
- Sessions usually take place weekly over a period of six to nine months.

Supportive psychotherapy
- Aims to provide regular reassurance, encouragement, and a degree of sympathy;
- Sessions are informal and take place less frequently than formal psychotherapy—perhaps once a month.

Behaviour therapy
- Believes that behaviour is 'learned' and can therefore be 'unlearned', or changed;
- Aims to stop you behaving in unhelpful or unwanted ways and to learn new patterns of behaviour that will make your life more enjoyable;
- Concentrates on how you behave at present and not on theories about why you learned to behave in certain ways.

Cognitive therapy
- Based on the theory that changes in our emotions and behaviour are determined by our thoughts about events that occur. If we always take a gloomy or frightened view of life, we will interpret everything that happens in a negative way;
- Aims to help you recognise and change unhelpful and gloomy ways of thinking;
- Incorporates some parts of behaviour therapy.

Counselling
- Aims to help you help yourself by understanding why you feel the way you do and by planning how to cope with emotional and practical realities;
- Helps you to live the life you have chosen by discussing current problems and alternative practical solutions;
- Provides a considerable amount of social support.

Family therapy
- Views you as a member of a family or similar social group;
- Is concerned with how the members of the family or group communicate with each other and with their relationships;

- Aims to resolve distress and conflict without apportioning blame by using various psychotherapeutic methods.

Group therapy
- A group of people who did not know each other before come together with a therapist to help each other with their problems;
- Groups may be made up of people with the same problem or different problems, and they may be single sex or mixed;
- Group members can see that they are not alone in having problems and can get a great deal of support from other members of the group.

Psychoanalysis
- Believes that our behaviour and mental state originate in early experiences in childhood;
- Different schools of psychoanalysis interpret the meaning of what you say differently;
- A great deal of time is taken up in discussing the relationship between you and the therapist—this is taken to represent the relationship between you and important people in your early life such as your mother or father;
- Psychotherapy sessions take place several times a week over a period of years and so the treatment can be costly in terms of both time and money.

Time—the great healer

Perhaps the most neglected treatment of all is time. A mild depressive illness can get better on its own, given time, and spontaneous recovery is known even in severe depression. Quite a lot of people do get better anyway, sometimes in spite of the treatment prescribed! Spontaneous improvement is most likely, however:
- In a first episode of depression;
- When the depressive illness started recently;
- When the illness started suddenly;
- Where depression is the result of a major stress;
- When you have relatives and friends who can give you practical and emotional support.

Who can help?

If you are worred about the way you feel, get help as soon as possible—if you are ill, the earlier treatment starts, the better. If your depression is mild, you may find that the very act of seeking help and discussing problems with your family or friends is useful and can help.

Ministers of religion

For many depressed people there is a natural tendency to turn to religion for solace and support. For those who believe, the strength of shared belief and the sense of belonging and common purpose can overcome adversity and demoralisation.

Ministers of religion usually have great experience in counselling and are often more than willing to talk things over and provide support.

Voluntary bodies

Voluntary bodies such as MIND (01 637 0741) and the Samaritans can provide a sympathetic ear, information and advice. The College of Health has a telephone help-line (01–980 4848), which provides tape recorded facts about a range of medical disorders, including depression. Where relationship problems are important, it may be useful to contact your local branch of Relate.

Psychiatric services within the NHS

For most people, the first professional contact is their GP. Often specialist help from psychiatrists, clinical psychologists, psycho-therapists and others in the NHS can only be obtained by a referral from your GP. Occasionally, specialists will agree to see you without a GP referral, but they will usually want to keep your GP aware of their involvement. If you want to see a specialist but for some reason can't get a referral it is worth getting in touch with your local hospital to find out if you can be seen by self referral. Psychiatric services, like others within the NHS, are under severe pressure. Most people are treated by their GP and if they are referred to a hospital specialist it can take some time before they are seen.

Seeing a psychiatrist privately

You can see a psychiatrist privately. This can be arranged by your GP, by making enquiries through the general manager at your local hospital, or by getting in touch with a local private psychiatric hospital or clinic.

Self referral

Because of pressure on hospital services and criticism that the traditional medical approach to the treatment of depression neglects personal and social aspects, there is an increasing number of voluntary and private 'self referral' agencies for people with depression—some within the NHS or run jointly with local authority social services departments. Details are usually available from your local community health council, citizen's advice bureau, social services department, library or community centre.

    Understanding Mental Health (Published by Which? Books) and *Someone to Talk to Directory* (published by the Mental Health Foundation) list a large number of organisations and sources of information and help. These books tell you how to contact various national organisations that can put you in touch with specialists (mostly non-medical) in counselling and psychotherapy, and should be available through your library. Some of these are voluntary or charitable bodies, others are private, and a charge is usually made for treatment.

A last word

Although we cannot avoid sadness, unhappiness and depression, we can learn to deal with these emotions and live with them successfully rather than letting them overwhelm us to the extent that they affect our mental and physical health adversely.

Because of the enormous individual differences in what causes depression and in our ability to cope with it, this booklet cannot hope to give the answer to everyone's problems. What it has tried to do, however, is to help you think about and identify undesirable depression in your own life and learn how to control it—either alone or with the help of others.

Taking stock of ourselves and our lives in this way from time to time can be an extremely beneficial exercise. It is amazing how little we question our priorities and how many sources of unnecessary depression we can be rid of by doing this.

Index